CLK: Nothing Serious, Just Love.

Arby B

BookLeaf Publishing

Presentation by *BookLeaf Publishing*

Web: www.bookleafpub.com

E-mail: info@bookleafpub.com

ISBN: 9789357211338

First edition 2022

DEDICATION

To CLK. Yesterday, today, tomorrow and the next day, I'll be here. Loving you.

ACKNOWLEDGEMENT

MSR. Thank you for always being my biggest cheerleader and most honest sounding board. I am so proud of you and I love you beyond measure. YOU and KJT are my sun, moon and stars.

PREFACE

Falling in love makes all the world poetry, makes every moment sweeter and makes people glow differently. For me, falling in love for the first time in a long time, has been an epic journey of self discovery and patience, compassion and bittersweet pain. I've always felt things with such an intensity that I needed to find an outlet. Writing is my outlet. Every morning over coffee. Every evening over wine. Words pour from my heart, bleed through my pen and stain blank pages every single day.

In my eyes, love and friendship are the same thing. Friend love is a deep respect and compassion for that person, mixed with honest communication and an enjoyment of their company. Romantic love is the same, but with extras like passion, physical intimacy and butterflies. I'm not the only one to ever struggle with dancing the line between the two.

I see you.

Sure.
I see your happiness,
your sadness,
your pain,
your fear.

Behind that,
I see your goodness,
strength,
compassion,
kindness,
creativity,
passion,
and beautiful soul.

What do I feel?

Butterflies on steroids.
Not a light fluttering at all.
More like a fucking rhinoceros with wings.
Every day since my heart
went rogue
against my better judgment.

I've never felt this before.
Butterflies, yes.
This,
whatever-the-fuck-rhinoceros,
no.
Never.

Maybe it's what love feels like,
after waking from a long dormant state?
Maybe it's what happens,
when an Aquarius meets a Leo?
Maybe it's when I look in your eyes,
I see you and appreciate you.

Maybe it's fear.
A deep knowing that
I'm falling,
hard and fast,

and I have no control over
how I land.

Cracking

I have loved my kids forever.
Loved myself for half that time.
Loved my life for a year.

I have not loved a man for five years.
I can feel my heart cracking open,
bursting, freaking the fuck out.

I'm terrified.

3:30 am

I woke up and rolled over.
My first thoughts were of you.
Sleeping, hopefully soundly.
Warm in your bed.

Wanting so much
to be able to touch your skin,
feel your hot nakedness,
my body pressed to yours.

But more than that,
wanting to feel your heart.
Fill in all the cracks and wounds,
and love you. Properly.

Knowing

I went to bed last night,
tears slowly trickling
down my face.

Woke at 3am,
a knot in my stomach,
tears behind my eyes.

You know I'm falling.
I know you can't love.
So what do I do?

Futile?

How do you fix
a heart that has
been shattered?
A heart turned cold?

You can't.
Love them anyway.

Is it futile?
Perhaps.

But it's the broken
that need to know,
maybe more than anyone,
that they are loved.

Authenticity

You are magic.
A whirlwind of
passion and fire,
mixed with
decency and goodness.

You are the most real
of anyone I've ever met.
And in your authenticity,
you speak your truth:
"I cannot love."

Makes me fall
farther and deeper
into the abyss
of wanting you,
of loving you.

Driving. Parking. Riding.

You sat in my passenger seat,
every nerve ending in my body,
awake and alive,
buzzing at your proximity.

So I drove.
Distracting my mind,
focusing on the road
and not your nearness.

Until I couldn't take any more.
I asked if I could sit on your lap.
You said "sure", I stopped breathing.
So I stopped driving.

Parked by the water, sitting on your lap,
our first kiss, looking into your eyes,
I have never in my life felt so intimate,
with my clothes still on.

Staying.

When I said
"I can meet you where you're at."
I meant,

I understand
that your heart is wounded
and you can't love.

But I care about you
more than walking away
from you.

That's the thing about love.
I don't care how much my heart might hurt,
I'm not going anywhere.

Until you tell me to.

White Flag.

Three days of not talking to you.
Depression. Alcohol. Distractions.
Propositions unmet.

Day four I woke up and
whispered to the Universe,
"I surrender."

Soul despair,
knot in my stomach.
Tears behind my eyes.

The Universe whispered back,
gently, quietly, on the breeze,
"Cory."

Cannot.

"I cannot love again."
You said it the first time
and I heard the words,
but I still fell in love with you.

"I cannot love again."
You said it the second time,
and I walked away for days.
but I tried not to love you.

"I cannot love again."
You said it the third time,
and I understood,
deeply, to my core.

You will love again.
And it won't be me.
But I'll still be here
loving you.

Explicit.

My head in your lap
between your legs
(my favorite place).

Your hand gently stroking
my hair, my neck
(sweetest memory).

Making love to you
with my mouth
(for the first time I love doing it).

It's the only way I have right now
to pour myself into you
(let me love you).

It's the only way I have right now
to drink you in
(so fucking good).

Brake.

My heart has only ever known one speed:
0 to love in 6.5 seconds.
The all or nothing love.

It's different with you.
All in? Yes. All pistons firing? Yes.
No. Brake. Slow down.
Full stop.

I care about you enough to slow down.
Be your friend.
Fully support whatever it is
that you need for you.

Even if it's not me.

Gravitational pull.

Like the moon
and the tide,
I ebb and flow
toward you, away from you.

Whatever you need in that moment:
space, love, time, support.
I ebb and flow,
toward you, away from you.

It's not for me.
The tide loves the moon either way.
I ebb and flow.
But always end up back

to you.

Hi.

You walked into my life
so casually.
I met your eyes with mine
and it was over.

Your goodness,
your brokenness,
your darkness and
your light.

All of you,
I want to absorb,
read, re-read,
understand.

Only
so that I can know
how to love you
better.

Eyes.

I wish you could,
just for a moment, see yourself
through my eyes.

Not just your
skin deep
gorgeousness,

but your vibe, your energy,
your honesty,
your goodness.

Sure. I see your "imperfections",
your broken pieces,
your wounds.

But you are so much
more
than that.

You are more
than your
brokenness.

So much more.
And I love
all of it.

Trees.

You know how you can look at a tree
and just appreciate it for what it is?
Just as it is, with no expectations?
You don't feel the need to change anything?

Broken limbs, healing scars
but still perfectly beautiful just rooted there
growing gently and slowly toward the light
doing its thing?

Yeah.
That's how I see you.

Happy. Thank you. More please.

You said "froth" at thick clumps of bubbles
floating in the tide.
I thought it was hot. But any words, out of your
mouth, are hot.
It made me want more. Of you.

I could talk to you for hours.
Telling me about your world, your past, your
present and your future.
And still be left wanting more. Of you.

I could sit on your lap, or on my knees,
imprinting my skin with rocks and railroad
spikes,
And still be left wanting more. Of you.

Daily Reminder

You are goodness.
The world needs you.
You are a fucking amazing human
and I'm so glad we met.
You have a gorgeous @!#&.
Your light far outshines your darkness.
You are not defined by what people say you are
(or are not).
You are a magical fucking Unicorn!
You are not at all difficult to love.
You are kind.
You are breathtaking.
You deserve a life that doesn't hurt and a love
that soothes your soul
(and a beej whenever you want).
I appreciate you.
I am excited when I see you and I miss you
when you're gone.
Thank you for being you.

PS: You are so smoking hot / you are hot af /
you are stunningly handsome!
Unsubscribe any time by texting STOP.

You do you.

Take the time to work on you.
Take as many years as you need
in order to feel whole and strong
and okay again.

Talk to as many women as you can.
Seduce them with your words,
with your beautiful heart and soul.
Let them all (every single one of them)
fall in love with you so you KNOW
that you are loveable.

They will (might) leave when their hope dies.
When they find out you won't love.
Be okay with that.
When you're ready, when your heart is
still broken but open to possibility,
you'll meet the one that you
won't want to live without.

That may be a year, it may be 10.
You do you. Without shame or guilt.

But understand that their leaving is NOT
because there is something wrong with you.

It's because there is something
so RIGHT

that they

can't

have.

Two words.

Nothing serious.
You said.
I fell in love with you.

Nothing serious.
I backed off and
love being your friend.

Nothing serious.
I still want you, painfully so.
I don't want you to think that I don't.
I do.
I want all of you.
I don't want to be
just friends.

But I won't push.
I won't beg.
I want to.
But I won't.
Ever (again).

Nothing serious.
Because that's what you want.
And because
I love you.

www.ingramcontent.com/pod-product-compliance
Lightning Source LLC
Chambersburg PA
CBHW051754130826
49812CB00033B/1141
* 9 7 8 9 3 5 7 2 1 1 3 3 8 *